A BLACKBIRCH NATURE BOOK

Animal Journeys
Life Cycles and Migrations

Susanne Riha

BLACKBIRCH PRESS, INC.
WOODBRIDGE, CONNECTICUT

Published by Blackbirch Press, Inc.
260 Amity Road
Woodbridge, CT 06525
web site: http://www.blackbirch.com
e-mail: staff@blackbirch.com

Printed in Belgium

10 9 8 7 6 5 4 3 2 1

First published in German as *Wir Machen eine weite Reise* by Annette
Betz Verlag, © 1998.

Library of Congress Cataloging-in-Publication Data
Riha, Susanne.
    [Wir machen eine weite reise. English].
    Animal journeys: migrations in nature / Susanne Riha.—1st ed.
        p. cm.
    "A Blackbirch nature book."
    Summary: Discusses the migratory habits of such animals as toads,
butterflies, blue whales, pink pelicans, and others.
    ISBN 1-56711-426-1
    1. Animal migration—Juvenile literature. [1. Animals—Migration.]
I. Title.
QL754.R5413   1999   99–13894
591.56'8—dc21   CIP

Contents

Toads

Toads are slow travelers. They need many days to complete their journeys from their forest to their hidden breeding places by a nearby pond. Most toads like to travel after the sun goes down—at dusk or nighttime.

Toads wake in the spring from their winter sleep, called hibernation. Together with many other toads, they begin a journey to their spawning (egg-laying) place. There, they will lay eggs and fertilize them. For the last part of this trip, the females actually carry the males!

Having arrived at a pond, the toads all rest. When they are ready, the females squeeze a sort of long transparent hose from their bodies. As they do, the males cling to the females and fertilize the eggs. The hose gets wrapped around the stems of the pond's plants. These hoses are filled with eggs.

Now the toads set out for their return trip. In the meantime, the sun will warm the eggs in the water and ripen them. After about two weeks, thousands of brand new tadpoles will be swimming around in the pond.

Because they breathe through gills (like fish), tadpoles can only live in the water. With tiny pointy teeth, they feed on water plants. Slowly their gills disappear and lungs develop. Legs start to grow and their long tails disappear. At this stage, a tadpole feeds mostly on insects. Finally, a small brownish toad crawls up on land and begins its first journey to the forest.

Size: Male, 4.7 in (12cm), female, 7.9 in (20cm)
Food: Insects, snails, and worms
Lifespan: Up to 15 years
Territory: All over the world, except extremely cold climates near North and South poles

White Butterflies

Butterflies are wandering, or migratory, insects. In the spring, if there are too many butterflies in one place, some of them will travel to a less crowded area. Some of them will even fly for hundreds of miles.

As soon as butterflies get the urge to migrate, their flight pattern changes. They no longer flutter gently back and forth over gardens and meadows. Instead, they only fly straight ahead. As they fly, one butterfly is right behind the other, as if they were tied together with an invisible string. That is how they fly over wide waters and high mountains.

At some point, the butterflies will stop. They may find a vegetable garden or other quiet patch. There, on the underside of large leaves (usually cabbage leaves) the female will deposit her eggs. Soon, the eggs hatch and small caterpillars crawl out onto the leaves.

These caterpillars are yellowish green with some black spots on their sides. They eat many leaves and grow very rapidly. Then, one day the caterpillar crawls up a tree onto a high branch. It attaches itself to the bark with silken threads that it spins around itself. Inside this cocoon, the caterpillar becomes an immobile "pupa."

After several weeks, the cocoon bursts open. A young butterfly stretches the first pair of its six legs out in front of itself. Finally, it sheds its cocoon completely and unfolds its wings for the very first time.

Wingspan: 2.3 in (4–6cm)
Food: Flower nectar, juice from overripe fruit
Lifespan: 1 year
Territory: Europe, North America, Asia

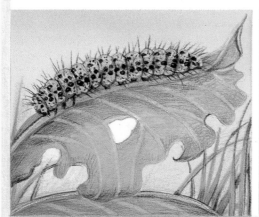

Salmon

Salmon journeys involve travels from freshwater (lakes and rivers) to saltwater (ocean) and then back again.

Salmon life begins in a river. Young salmon, called fry, hatch from thousands of eggs.

At two years of age, a salmon swims downriver into the ocean. There, it learns to hunt for fish.

Salmon reach full adulthood several years later. Then, instinct draws them back to their place of birth. Incredibly, they can remember the scent of their river. They actually find their way back with their sense of smell! At the mouth of the river they meet up with other salmon that share the same birthplace.

Crowded tightly together, the group swims upstream. In order to overcome many obstacles—including strong currents—the salmon jump out of the water and skim over the river. Only their tail fins stay in the water. With strong strokes, the salmon propel themselves forward. With each jump they can move about 1.5 feet (.5 meter). When they are back at their place of birth, the males fight for a chance to mate with the females.

The female spawns (lays eggs) in shallow water on the river banks. With her tail fin she makes a hole in the sand. There, she lays her eggs and covers them.

The salmon have not eaten since leaving the ocean. After spawning—even though they are exhausted—they head back to the ocean.

Size: Up to 5 ft (1.5m)
Weight: Up to 77 lbs (35kg)
Food: Insects, crabs, fish
Lifespan: Up to 6 years
Territory: Throughout rivers and the Atlantic and Pacific oceans

Pink Pelicans

Pink pelicans do everything together. They live together in big colonies. They like to eat and rest together. In the fall, as the weather turns cold, they take off together on a long trip to the south. As they fly in a neat V-formation, their wings even beat together in unison.

Pink pelicans are long-distance flyers with incredible strength. To rest, they will stop at a large body of water. There, they swim close to each other and form a semi-circle. This way, they round up groups of small fish for a meal.

When the warm spring weather returns, the colony flies back to cooler climates. There, they build their nests, usually at the mouth of a large river.

A pink pelican's nest is a simple hollowed-out area in the rushes or reeds. Here, the females and males take turns incubating (sitting on and warming) the eggs. It's quiet in the pelican colony before all the babies are born. Soon there will be many young pelicans begging for food. Their parents will need to set out on fishing trips to find food for their young. In order to find enough food for all the newborn pelicans, the adults often have to fly great distances. The large, flexible pouches under their beaks come in handy for carrying all the fish they need.

While their parents are fishing, the young pelicans are left hidden among the reeds, quietly and eagerly awaiting their parents' return.

Size: 5 ft (1.5m)
Weight: 22 lbs (10kg)
Food: Fish
Lifespan: 40 years • ⚠ Endangered
Territory: Donau delta to India, Egypt, Africa

Sea Turtles

One of the largest sea turtles is the green turtle. These reptiles used to be hunted by humans for food. Today the species is endangered and is protected by laws. Green sea turtles feed on sea grass along the coasts and like to doze in shallow waters.

At certain times, sea turtles will drastically change their daily behaviors. They set out on a long journey, returning to their place of birth. Often, this journey takes them thousands of miles away from their feeding grounds. But somehow, they know the way. As they arrive, males and females gather and meet each other.

After mating, the female slowly crawls up on land. As she moves, she makes a big trail in the sand. She stops when she finds a private spot in which to lay her eggs. She digs a hole and places her tail inside. Within a half hour, she deposits up to 200 eggs. She then covers the nest with sand and pounds the earth with her shell to pack it down and make it solid.

The eggs ripen (incubate) in the warm sand while the female sea turtles begin their journeys back to their feeding grounds. Finally, they arrive, exhausted and hungry.

After two months, the little turtles hatch and crawl out of the sand. Within minutes, they make their way to the water, trying to avoid condors and other predators.

Five years later, the young turtles become adults. Then, they too will journey back to their birthplace.

Size: Up to 4 ft (1.2m) (shell)
Weight: Up to 440 lbs (200kg)
Food: Sea grass, seaweed, algae, fish, crabs
Lifespan: Up to 100 years • ⚠ Endangered
Territory: Atlantic, Caribbean, Pacific, Indian oceans

African Elephants

Herds of elephants will often travel through the night, quietly making their way through the vast African grasslands (savanna). During their travels the elephants cross almost all of Africa's savanna. And they always follow the exact same path—often called an elephant street. After three years of travel they come back to their starting point.

During a lengthy trip, they will stop at a familiar watering hole to drink, splash, and bathe. Most herds consist only of females and young elephants. An experienced older female leads the herd—about 50 animals.

The males, or bulls, roam on their own. Some form their own herds. Only at mating time do the males and females get together.

Life in the female herd is caring and social. The animals like to help each other and to make physical contact. They help clean each other, and when an animal is wounded, herd members will close the wound with mud.

A female elephant gives birth only every four years. When she is ready, the other females form a circle around her. One female helps with the delivery. As soon as the newborn can walk, the mother and calf join the herd again.

A newborn elephant is a bit hairy. It is about 3 feet (1 meter) tall and weighs about 265 pounds (120 kilograms). A large baby by animal standards, this newborn is still small enough to walk under its mother's belly!

Size: Male, up to 12.5 ft (3.8m), Female, up to 9.2 ft (2.8m)
Weight: Male, up to 7 tons, Female, up to 4.5 tons
Food: Plants (herbivorous)
Lifespan: Up to 60 years • ⚠ Endangered
Territory: Africa; south of the Sahara desert

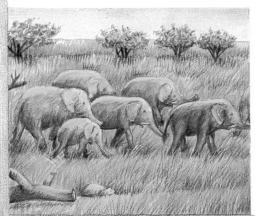
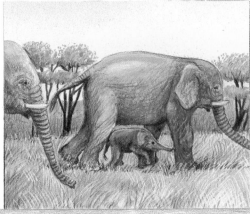

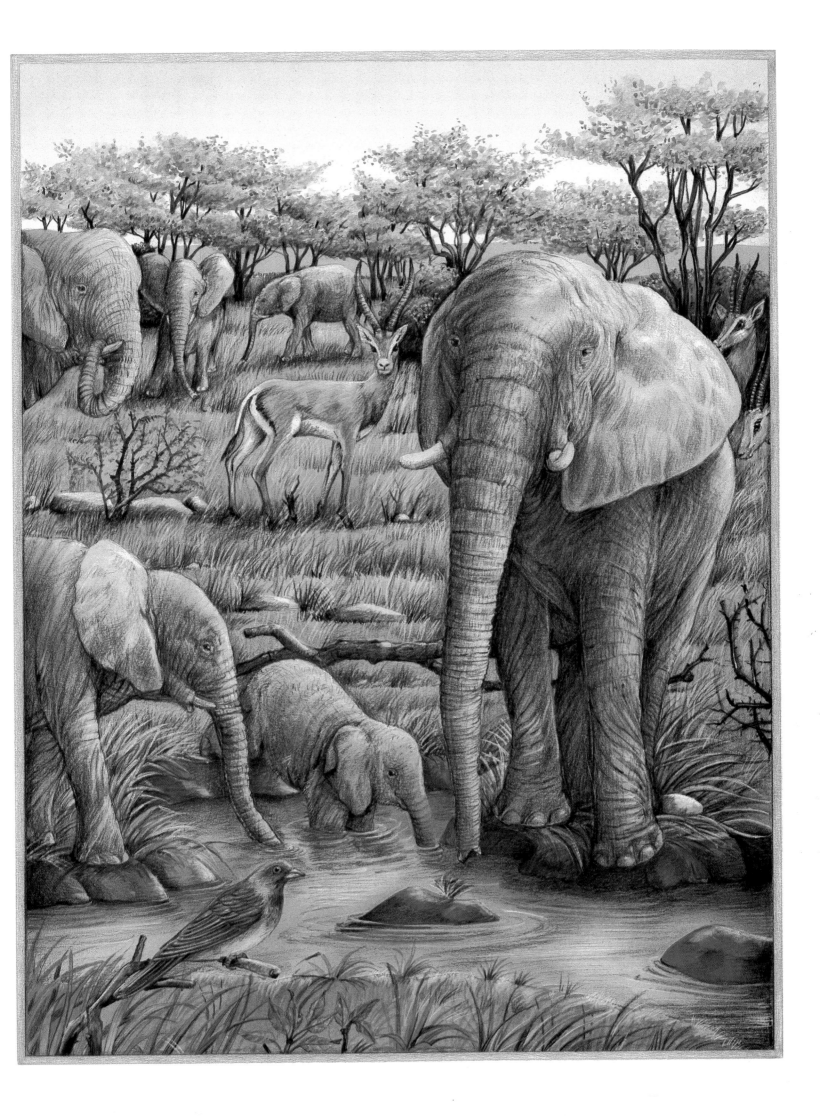

Locusts

A swarm of locusts can move into an area in the blink of an eye. Within just a few moments of their arrival, every leaf, flower, and blade of grass will be consumed, leaving nothing.

Sometimes, a swarm can measure more than 60 or 70 square miles (up to 200 square kilometers). Large swarms can number in the millions, or even billions (the largest swarm ever was 10 billion!).

Most locusts travel distances of more than 1,500 miles (2,500 kilometers). Desert locusts will travel (migrate) farther than any other insect. Some of these creatures have been known to travel more than 3,000 miles (5,000 kilometers) across the entire Atlantic Ocean!

Locusts can reproduce all year long. In order to lay eggs, the female pushes the back of her body into the ground until she feels moist soil. Then she deposits up to 100 eggs, each about the size of a grain of rice.

After a few weeks, the larvae crawl to the surface. About 7 days later, they crawl up a tree, and hang upside down from a branch. Then they inflate themselves until the skin at the back of their heads cracks open and they can crawl out. After a few more sheddings (molts) the larvae soon develop into green or grey wingless 'hoppers.' With their strong thighs, the hoppers can make long jumps over land. Eventually, swarms of winged locusts gather and take off together in search of food.

Size: 2.8 in (7cm) • Wingspan: 6 in (15cm)
Food: Plants, grass, leaves
Lifespan: Up to 1 year
Territory: Wide ranging; throughout Africa, India, North and South America

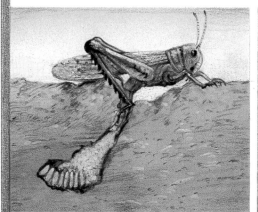

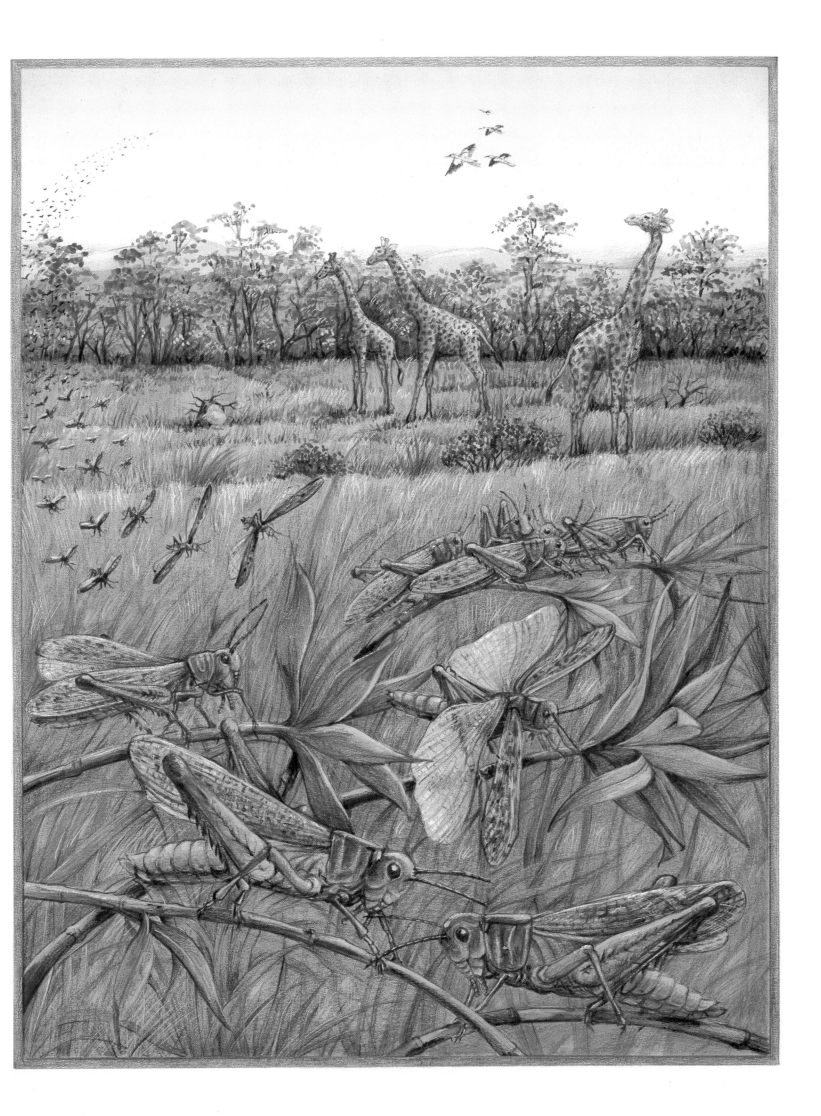

Arctic Terns

Of all animal journeys, the Arctic terns cover the greatest distance. In the spring, a female flies from the South Pole to the North Pole. In the fall, she travels back to the South Pole. In the polar regions, when the nights are light, these birds can search for food almost constantly.

Arctic terns travel mostly along coastlines. Their journeys are often dangerous. Storms may blow them far over the ocean and fog may cause them to lose their direction.

Terns will often pause at the mouths of big rivers. There, they can feed on insects and dive for fish.

By May, an Arctic tern reaches the most northern coasts. Now, the fight for a nesting place begins. Each mating pair battles others for the place they had the previous year.

An Arctic tern's nest is simply a dug-out area in the sand. Males and females share the job of keeping the three to four eggs warm. After four weeks, the grey-brown chicks hatch. In order to survive, they need to be fed by their parents. The adults spend much time hunting for fish and bringing them back to the nest.

When the chicks leave their nest, they have to be careful not to walk too close to a neighbor's nest. Parent terns are very protective of their young. If a chick gets too close, it could be pecked to death.

At several weeks of age, the young Arctic terns make their first long journey back to the South Pole.

Size: 2 ft (38cm)
Weight: 8 oz (250g)
Food: Fish, shrimp, insects
Lifespan: Up to 10 years
Territory: North to South poles

Blue Whales

Blue whales live their whole lives in the sea. Most will travel a total of 10,500 miles (17,000 kilometers) in a year. With a body length of up to 98 feet (30 meters), the blue whale is the largest living mammal on Earth.

The strong tail fin (caudal fin) propels the whale's huge body through the water. Every five minutes, a whale surfaces to breathe. Through openings on top of its head (blowholes), a whale blows a large cloud of spray into the air. Different species of whales can be identified by the unique shape of their geysers.

Blue whales feed on tiny shrimp-like crustaceans called krill. A blue whale can filter about 3 to 4 tons of krill through its large mouth each day.

Krill live in the ice-cold polar seas. In the fall, when the water starts to freeze, blue whales begin their journey south to warmer waters along the coasts of Africa and Asia.

In warmer waters, the females give birth to their young. A newborn calf is about 23 feet (7 meters) long and weighs about 2 tons. Like other mammals, the baby nurses on milk from its mother. Calves can gain about 220 pounds (100 kilograms) per day! Eventually, they swim back to the North Pole with their mothers.

Blue whales usually travel in groups of three or four called pods. If one loses its way, it will call to the others using high-frequency sound waves much like those of bats and dolphins.

Size: 98 ft (30m)
Weight: 150 tons
Food: Crabs, shrimp, tiny crustaceans, plankton
Lifespan: About 30 years • ⚠ Endangered
Territory: From North or South poles to the equator

Greylag Geese

In the fall, greylag geese are found in the harvested fields of Europe. They search for clover, dandelions, and kernels of grain. While most geese feed, a few keep watch.

Over the winter they stay in Europe. When the weather turns warmer, they travel for thousands of miles to the far north.

Male and female greylag geese pair off for at least a year before they build a nest. Once they pair off, however, males and females stay together for their life-time. While the female sits on the eggs, the male stands guard nearby. After 4 weeks, up to 9 chicks will hatch. Greylag geese are good parents. They show their chicks the best feeding places and bring them to water. Greylag males are good protectors and will defend the chicks at all costs. After 2 months, a chick's feathers turn grey and the legs as well the beaks become orange colored.

This is also the time to learn to fly. Soon the young geese fly as well as their parents do. A greylag goose can fly up to 20,000 feet (6,000 meters) high. On their long journeys, they fly through the day and night. A group, or squadron, of greylag geese is usually led by an experienced female.

Young greylag geese will accompany their parents when they fly south in the fall, returning to Europe. But their desire to travel is not inborn. Instead, it is taught by copying their parents' behavior.

Size: 3 ft (90cm) • Weight: up to 2.2 lbs (10kg)
Food: Grass, leaves, sprout or shoots from clover and dandelions, herbs, roots, berries, grains, tubers
Lifespan: Up to 40 years
Territory: From the Arctic tundra to southern Europe

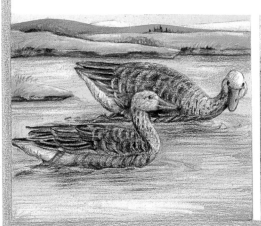

Ibex

When the first snowfall comes to the high mountains, the ibex (mountain goats) begin their journey into the valley. On the same worn path they have used for generations, they climb down the rocky mountainside. Ibex are excellent climbers. Their hooves, which are like suction cups, enable them to keep their footing, even on very steep cliffs. The hooves have a hard outer rim and are hollow on the inside.

The male ibex has a beard and two large horns. The horns might be up to 3 feet (1 meter) long. In the fall, the horn's brown fur turns grey.

After a long journey down the mountain, the males arrive at the forest. Here, they meet the females. They also begin to fight with other males over the females. During the winter, the males and females stay together in the forest. When spring arrives, they begin their climb back up into the mountains. Many females climb a bit higher up the mountains during the summer. There, alone, they give birth to their young.

After just a few days, a young goat is strong enough—and sure-footed enough—to accompany its mother back to the herd. Nearly every day during spring, a new baby ibex joins the herd. When all the young are born, a kind of "ibex children's group" is formed. One of the mothers takes on the responsibility of leading all the young as they travel.

Size: 2.3 ft (70cm) (shoulder height)
Weight: Up to 265 lbs (120kg)
Food: Herbs, buds, moss, vines
Lifespan: 15 years • Protected
Territory: Alps, high mountains of Europe, Asia

Reindeer

Reindeer herds spend their summers in the far north, on the treeless tundra. There, they find enough mosses, lichens, and grasses to survive. When snow begins to fall, they must make their way south, back to the forests.

The herd stops to eat and rest frequently on its journey. As they travel, a reindeer mother keeps careful watch while her young reindeer eats. If she needs to, she will use her large horns to defend her family. The horns of an adult have many branches. Two of them are smoothed out and shaped like shovels.

Reindeer are well outfitted for their long travels. They have thick fur and are good swimmers. While walking on mud or snow, their hooves can spread far apart so they don't sink too deep.

A reindeer can travel about 62 miles (100 kilometers) per day. Their complete journey from the tundra to the forest can be a total distance of more than 620 miles (1,000 kilometers). When they finally enter the protection of the forest, they remain there for the winter. In the forest, many new reindeer will be born. A newborn can stand within only an hour of birth.

When it is ready, a young reindeer joins the herd with its mother. The mother reindeer continues to nurse her young for half a year.

In the spring, the reindeer leave the forest and travel the same road back to their fields on the tundra.

Size: 5 ft (1.5m) (shoulder height)
Weight: Up to 660 lbs (300kg)
Food: Mosses, grasses, lichen
Lifespan: Up to 20 years
Territory: Northern tundra to southern Asia, Europe

Glossary

Cocoon—a covering made from silky threads produced by some animals to protect themselves or their eggs.

Colony—a group of families or members that live together and help each other in some way.

Fertilize—with eggs, when male sperm joins with female eggs to create the new beginning of life.

Gills—blood-filled organs used for breathing underwater.

Hibernate—to spend the winter in a deep sleep to survive low temperatures and lack of food.

Incubate—to keep eggs warm so they will hatch.

Larva—an insect in the stage of development between egg and pupa when it looks like a worm.

Migration—animals moving from one place to another at a certain time of year or a certain stage of their life cycle.

Migratory—see migration.

Molt—to shed outer skin in order to make room for a new, larger layer.

Pod—a group of whales that live, swim, and feed together.

Pupa—insect in the development stage between larva and adult.

Pupae—plural of pupa.

Savanna—a flat, grassy plain with few or no trees.

Spawn—to release a large number of eggs.

Tundra—a cold area of northern Europe and Asia where there are no trees and the soil under the surface of the ground is permanently frozen.

For More Information

Books

Bennett, Paul. *Migration* (Nature's Secrets). New York, NY: Thomson Learning, 1994.

Gans, Ron. Paul Mirocha (Illustrator). *How Do Birds Find Their Way?* (Let's Read and Find Out Science). New York, NY: HaperCollins Children's Books, 1996.

King, Deborah. *The Flight of the Snow Geese*. New York, NY: Orchard Books, 1998.

Lepthien, Emilie U. *Sea Turtles* (True Books). Danbury, CT: Children's Press, 1996.

Riley, Helen. *Frogs and Toads*. New York, NY: Thomson Learning, 1993.

Simon, Seymour. Elsa Warnick (Illustrator). *They Swim The Seas: The Mystery of Animal Migration*. Orlando, FL. Browndeer Press, 1998.

Web Sites

African Elephants
Learn more about this endangered species and listen to the noises they make—ils.unc.edu/nczoo/eleph.html

Australian Koala Foundation
Find information on the life cycle, history, eating habits, behavior, and communications of these interesting marsupials—www.akfkoala.gil.com.au/koala.html

Index